pinpoint

ENGLISH

grammar and punctuation

Y4

Contents

    Pinpoint English Grammar and Punctuation Year 4/P5

Glossary

adverbial: a word or group of words that acts as an adverb describing how, where or when something happened

formal language: the language you would use in a formal situation, for example a speech or an important letter

fronted adverbial: a group of words at the start of a sentence that shows how, where or when something is happening

indent: leaving a space on the line before you write the first word

inverted commas: punctuation marks used to show direct speech (sometimes called speech marks)

irregular: a word that does not follow the rule

non-Standard English: language that is grammatically incorrect and includes slang and dialect words

noun: a word used to name a place, a person, a thing, or an idea, for example: *leg, Scotland, woman, sadness*

noun phrase: a group of words containing a noun and other words that add information about it, for example: *the tall boy with the dark hair*

paragraph: a group of sentences that are linked by topic, time or place

plural: more than one of something, for example: *cows*

possession: who or what owns something

possessive pronoun: a pronoun that can take the place of a noun with an apostrophe to show possession

preposition: a word that links a noun, pronoun or noun phrase to other words in the sentence, for example: *on, after, because of*

pronoun: a word that can take the place of a noun, for example: *he, him, they, us*

reporting clause: the words that tell the reader who is speaking, for example: *he said* or *said Alice*

singular: one of something, for example: *cow*

Standard English: formal or informal language that is grammatically correct and does not include slang and dialect words

verb: a word used to name an action or a state, for example: *jump, be, happen*

How does it work?

Pinpoint English Grammar and Punctuation uses elements of **scaffolded practice** to help children become confident in using correct grammar and punctuation. Each unit follows a familiar, structured approach and has a page of child-friendly answers with helpful reinforcement so that everyone can feel comfortable working independently.

1 Rule

The first page in each unit has a short, accessible introduction to the grammar or punctuation rule and any exceptions to it. You could read through this together with children, asking them to explain how the examples fit the rule.

Any technical terms are explained in the *abc* box below, enabling all children to access the unit. This will also allow parents and teachers to support learning.

The second page provides accessible questions to help children begin to explore the rule independently.

Even children with low confidence will feel supported when working on this page, thanks to highly structured, selected-response questions and hints from the Pinpoint children.

Used in conjunction with the first page of the unit, these activities help children work towards the expected standard.

2 Towards

3 Securing

The third page provides more challenging questions to encourage greater independence.

Children will explore the rule and put it into practice in short, constructed responses. Again, the Pinpoint children are on hand to provide support and encourage a positive mindset when faced with more difficult tasks.

Start here with more confident children who are working at the expected standard.

The final page provides longer activities that challenge children to think about the rule in context.

Children will be presented with a text correction activity, followed by a writing challenge where they must write a specific type of text using the rule from the unit. Some topic ideas will be provided, but children can draw on their own experiences and interests too.

This is not only a chance for children to consolidate their learning of the unit's grammar or punctuation rule, but also an opportunity to be creative and practise writing for a range of purposes.

4 Deeper

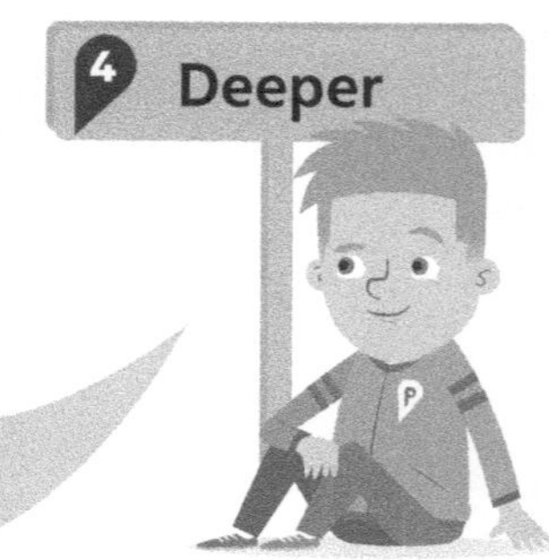

   Pinpoint English Grammar and Punctuation Year 4/P5

Top tips for grammar and punctuation success

Children can often feel like there are two options: you are a good at grammar or punctuation or you are bad at it. That needn't be the case. There are lots of ways that children can boost their grammar and punctuation confidence. Here are some tips for you to share with your class.

❶ Read more

One of many reasons to encourage a love of reading is to improve grammar and punctuation skills. Reading widely helps children to see accurate grammar and punctuation in practice and to know when a construction 'looks right'. Explain to children that this isn't about *guessing* whether a construction is correct, but is an important skill gained through experience and understanding of language.

When reading as a class or listening to individual readers, encourage children to match their voices to the clues in the punctuation (e.g. pause at a comma, raise pitch at a question mark), and stop occasionally to talk about interesting sentence structures or other grammar features.

❷ Make your own rule book

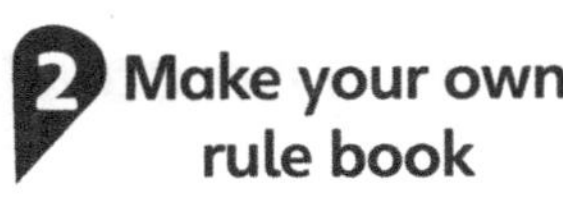

Children could create their own personal rule book using an exercise book or a notepad. Every time they come across a grammar or punctuation rule that they don't understand or struggle to get right, they can add it to their rule book, along with an example sentence or aid (such as a mnemonic, a picture or a rhyme).

Each grammar or punctuation rule in this book is clearly explained on the first page of the unit, but asking children to write their own explanation is a great way to develop and secure their understanding.

❸ Know your ABCs

The English language is notoriously complex, so it is not surprising that children may sometimes feel frustrated or overwhelmed by the rules. Begin your lessons with grammar and punctuation games to enable them to become familiar with common rules and terms, and to practise using them in a fun, relaxed context.

- Play grammar and punctuation bingo to help children learn new terminology. The cards can feature anything from basic punctuation marks to examples of tenses or sentence structures.

- Play charades to demonstrate how adverbs work. Make a set of verb cards and a set of adverb cards. A volunteer chooses a verb card and then silently acts it out for others to guess. When the correct answer has been guessed, they then choose an adverb card and silently act out the verb again, this time modified by the adverb.

- Get creative with mystery sentences. Give each child a piece of paper. Name an element of a sentence and ask the children to secretly write down an example at the top of their paper. Then ask them to fold their example backwards to hide it and pass the paper to their neighbour. Then, name another sentence element and again ask the children to write down an example at the top of the paper. When you have named enough elements to form a full sentence, ask each child to unfold their paper to reveal their mystery sentence and then check whether it is correct. You could read any funny ones aloud!

Plural and possessive *s*

Rule

To change a singular noun into a plural noun, you usually add *s*.

- *The* **cow** *was in the field.*

  one *cow* (singular)

- *The* **cows** *were in the field.*

  more than one *cow* (plural)

Add an apostrophe and *s* to singular nouns to show possession.

- *The* **cow's** *horns looked sharp.*

  more than one *horn* belonging to one *cow*

abc

singular: one of something, for example: *cow*

plural: more than one of something, for example: *cows*

possession: who or what owns something

   Pinpoint English Grammar and Punctuation Year 4/P5

Name ______________________________

Class ______________________________

Underline the plurals

1. The spider's webs stretched across the blades of grass.

2. The raindrops raced down the house's windows.

3. The castle's walls are twenty metres tall.

4. The dogs have chewed the table's legs.

5. The cat's whiskers twitched.

Add an apostrophe to show possession

1. There were strange noise☐s coming from our car☐s engine.

2. A lion☐s roar can be heard from a distance of five mile☐s.

3. My mum☐s earring☐s are made of coloured bead☐s.

4. The tree☐s leave☐s fly through the air on windy autumn day☐s.

5. The dog☐s muddy paw print☐s went all the way up the stair☐s.

There are some possessives and some plurals in these sentences. Think about which words show **who** or **what** something belongs to.

    Pinpoint English Grammar and Punctuation Year 4/P5

Name _______________________

Class _______________________

Correct the apostrophes

1 *Amys shoe's were much too small for her feet.*

2 *Some of Britains river's are very polluted with plastic.*

3 *The tyre's on Millie's bicycle are flat.*

4 *My sister's friend's are all going to Adils party.*

5 *My schools computer's were going very slowly in today's lessons.*

Use an apostrophe to rewrite...

1 *the ears belonging to the rabbit.*

____

2 *the boots belonging to the football player.*

____

3 *the car belonging to the teacher.*

____

4 *The garden belonging to our neighbour is much tidier than our garden.*

____

5 *There was a smile on the face belonging to the girl when her team won.*

____

     Pinpoint English Grammar and Punctuation Year 4/P5

D

Name _______________________

Class _______________________

Correct the apostrophes

This character description uses lots of imaginative language and descriptive detail but its apostrophes are missing or in the wrong place.

Cross out all of the incorrect apostrophes.
Then add the correct apostrophes.

The twins had hair as black and shiny as a ravens feathers. Both had dark eye's that twinkled, and long hair flowing down their back's, almost reaching their waists.

When they played, their laughter echoed through the house. They would shriek and scream at the top of their voice's. It always brought a smile to their mums' face.

Sometimes, though, there would be complete silence when the twin's were in their bedroom. This filled their mums mind with worrying thought's. She always wondered what they were up to.

Sometimes the twins would play tricks on their mother. They would wear each others clothes and pretend to be the other twin. Their trick's never fooled their mother though. She knew them too well.

Write your own description

Now that you have perfected the character description, write a description of a different character in your book. Use at least three plurals and three possessive apostrophes in your writing.

　　　Pinpoint English Grammar and Punctuation Year 4/P5　　　**9**

Possessive apostrophes with plural nouns

Rule

To show possession when a noun is plural and already ends in *s*, you just add an apostrophe.

- *The **rabbits' ears** were long and pointy.*

  more than one *ear* belonging to more than one *rabbit*

- *The **rhinos' legs** were like tree trunks.*

  more than one *leg* belonging to more than one *rhino*

Not all plurals end in *s*. These are called irregular plurals, for example:

one woman	two women
one man	two men
one child	two children

To show possession in an irregular plural, you add an apostrophe and *s*.

- *The **children's** voices were noisy.*

  more than one *voice* belonging to more than one *child*

abc

plural: more than one of something, for example: *cows*

possession: who or what owns something

irregular: a word that does not follow the rule

      Pinpoint English Grammar and Punctuation Year 4/P5

Name _______________________

Class _______________________

Match the noun phrase to the rewritten version

1 the beady eyes belonging to the eagles   the eagle's beady eyes

the beady eyes belonging to the eagle   the eagles' beady eyes

2 the long ears belonging to the donkey   the donkeys' long ears

the long ears belonging to the donkeys   the donkey's long ears

3 the sharp claws belonging to the tiger   the tiger's sharp claws

the sharp claws belonging to the tigers   the tigers' sharp claws

4 the hairy legs belonging to the spiders   the spider's hairy legs

the hairy legs belonging to the spider   the spiders' hairy legs

Circle another way to write …

1 the singing of the birds.

the birds' singing   the bird's singing   the birds singing

2 the smell belonging to the flowers.

the flower's smell   the flowers smell   the flowers' smell

3 the barking of the dogs.

the dogs barking   the dogs' barking   the dog's barking

4 lives belonging to people.

peoples' lives   peoples live's   people's lives

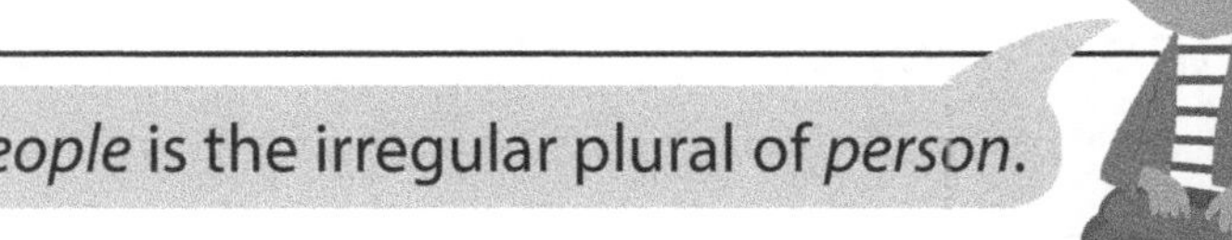

S **Name** _______________________

Class _______________________

Correct the apostrophes

1 _The childrens' packed lunches were delicious and very healthy._

2 _Four hungry horse's heads peered at me over the top of the bushes'._

3 _I spilt a glass of water on both my parent's phone's._

4 _Some womens' hats blew away in the high wind's._

5 _The buse's wheel's went round and round._

Some apostrophes are in the wrong place and some are not needed at all!

Write your own sentence about ...

1 _the smelly fumes belonging to the lorries._ Use a plural and a possessive apostrophe.

____

____

2 _the scooters belonging to the children._ Use a plural and a possessive apostrophe.

____

3 _the toys belonging to the cats._ Use a plural and a possessive apostrophe.

____

4 _the leaves on the tree._ Use a plural and a possessive apostrophe.

____

     Pinpoint English Grammar and Punctuation Year 4/P5

D **Name** _______________________

Class _______________________

Correct the apostrophes

This newspaper article gives the reader lots of information but all its apostrophes are in the wrong place!

Circle all of the incorrect apostrophes in one colour. Then add the correct apostrophes in a second colour.

School Bans Crisps and Chocolate

Wettington School in Northendshire has banned children from bringing crisps and chocolate to school in their packed lunches. The school wants to improve the student's health and encourage good eating habits.

The headteacher, Ms Glenn, has said that she gathered all the teacher's opinions before announcing the ban. "All the teacher's agree that chocolate is bad for the childrens' teeth and bad for the childrens' health," said Ms Glenn.

Some of the student's parents are very happy with the decision. Other parents are not so happy.

"We think we should decide what goes in our childrens' packed lunches," said one parent. "We think the school should listen to the parent's opinions and change their minds."

Write your own newspaper article

Now that you have perfected the newspaper article, write your own newspaper article in your book about a school that has introduced an unusual new subject. Use at least three possessive apostrophes with plural nouns in your writing.

Rule

The following grammar and punctuation rules are covered in this revision unit.

1 To make most singular nouns plural, you add *s*.

one cupcake   *three cupcakes*

2 Some nouns have irregular plurals.

one child   *two children*

one sheep   *two sheep*

one mouse   *two mice*

3 To show possession, you usually add an apostrophe and *s* to the noun.

*The **children's** parents waved happily.*

4 If the noun is plural and already ends in *s*, you just add an apostrophe to show possession.

*The **boys'** dinner was ready.*

abc

singular: one of something, for example: *cow*

plural: more than one of something, for example: *cows*

possession: who or what owns something

irregular: a word that does not follow the rule

      Pinpoint English Grammar and Punctuation Year 4/P5

T Name _______________________

Class _______________________

Circle the correct use of …

1 the plural.

womans   women   woman's

2 the plural.

mouses   mouse's   mice

3 an apostrophe for possession.

the women's clothes   the women' clothes   the womens' clothes

4 an apostrophe for possession.

the mouse's cheese   the mouse' cheese   the mouses cheese

5 an apostrophe for possession.

the people's voices   the peoples' voices   the peoples voices

Add an apostrophe to show possession

1 It was Mel☐s first day at her new school so her stomach was full of butterflie☐s and her palm☐s were sweating.

2 As she watched her parents☐car disappear into the distance, she felt tear☐s welling up in her eye☐s.

3 Mel saw huge crowd☐s of boy☐s and girl☐s, but she did not know anybody☐s name.

4 Then she saw two girls☐faces☐smiling at her and all her feelings☐of fear were gone.

Name _______________________

Class _______________________

Complete the sentences using these words

skateboards   skateboards'   skateboard's

girls   girl's   girls'

1 The _______________ set off for the park on their _______________.

2 Their _______________ wheels clattered over the pavement.

3 The _______________ chattering voices could be heard for miles around.

4 Suddenly, one _______________ skateboard skidded to a halt.

5 One of her _______________ wheels had come off!

Rewrite the underlined words using an apostrophe for possession

1 The rays of the sun shone through the leaves of the trees.

_______________   _______________

2 The ball flew off the boot belonging to Mari and sailed into the goal belonging to the other team.

_______________   _______________

3 The flames of the fire warmed the frozen toes belonging to Tom.

_______________   _______________

4 The petals of the flower slowly opened one bright day in summer.

_______________   _______________

        Pinpoint English Grammar and Punctuation Year 4/P5

Name _______________________

Class _______________________

Correct the apostrophes

This story opening uses lots of imaginative language but all its apostrophes are missing!

Add the apostrophes in the correct places.

The Magicians House

The houses walls were made of grey stone. Thick, green ivy climbed over them and curled itself around the windows. Thin puffs of smoke rose from the houses tall chimney and hovered in the air like tufts of sheeps wool.

Jeanie and Jim knocked quietly on the door. Soon they heard someones footsteps approaching. The doors hinges creaked and a little man stood smiling at them. His eyes were dark black, his eyebrows were pure white and on each of his shoulders sat a parrot.

"Good morning," said one of the mans parrots.

"Good morning," said the other parrot.

The childrens eyes widened in surprise. The two parrots four beady eyes watched them closely.

Continue the story

Now that you have perfected the beginning of the story, continue it in your book. Use at least three apostrophes of possession in your writing.

Standard English

Rule

People often use non-Standard English when they speak, but in most writing and in formal speech you should use Standard English. In Standard English, verbs change depending on who or what is doing the action they describe. For example,

I **was**
You **were**
She **was** — bouncing on the trampoline.
We **were**
They **were**

I **go**
You **go**
He **goes** — higher and higher on the trampoline.
We **go**
They **go**

---

abc

verb: a word used to name an action or a state, for example: *jump*, *be*, *happen*

Standard English: formal or informal language that is grammatically correct and does not include slang and dialect words

non-Standard English: language that is grammatically incorrect and includes slang and dialect words

formal language: the language you would use in a formal situation, for example a speech or an important letter

    Pinpoint English Grammar and Punctuation Year 4/P5

Name _______________________

Class _______________________

Match the answers

1 We were late.   Standard English

We was late.   non-Standard English

2 You was early.   Standard English

You were early.   non-Standard English

3 They was running.   Standard English

They were running.   non-Standard English

4 He was walking quickly.   Standard English

He were walking quickly.   non-Standard English

5 I was walking quickly.   Standard English

I were walking quickly.   non-Standard English

Circle the correct Standard English verb form

1 I go out.   I goes out.   I going out.

2 She go in.   She going in.   She goes in.

3 We say sorry.   We says sorry.   We was saying sorry.

4 We have done it.   We done it.   We has done it.

5 We was busy.   You was busy.   He was busy.

S **Name** ___________________________

Class ___________________________

Complete the sentence using a Standard English verb form

1 *We went to the cinema and watched a film which _______________ really good.*

2 *After the film, we _______________ hungry so we went for a pizza.*

3 *We did not order a dessert because we _______________ completely full!*

4 *Then my little sister started crying because she _______________ so tired.*

5 *I _______________ to my mum, "We should have left her at home!"*

> You will need to use forms of the verbs *be* (for example, *was* and *were*) and *say*.

Use Standard English to rewrite ...

1 *I were so happy reading my book!*

____

2 *The sun were shining.*

____

3 *There weren't a cloud in the sky.*

____

4 *The birds was singing in the trees.*

____

  Pinpoint English Grammar and Punctuation Year 4/P5

D Name _______________

Class _______________

Correct the verbs

Ben's postcard to his teacher is full of interesting details about his trip to London, but he has not written it in Standard English.

Underline all the non-Standard English verbs. Then add the Standard English verb form for each one.

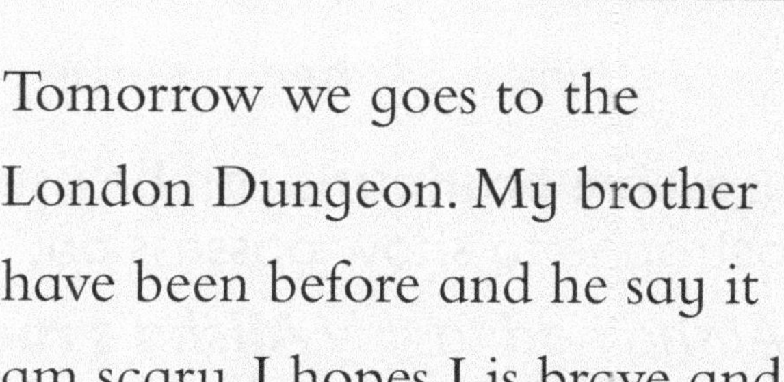

Dear Mrs Habib,

We is having an amazing time in London. We has been to the Tower of London, which were interesting, and the London Eye, which were really exciting. When you is at the top of the London Eye, you sees the whole of London and all the people below looks like tiny ants!

Tomorrow we goes to the London Dungeon. My brother have been before and he say it am scary. I hopes I is brave and does not start screaming.

I is looking forward to seeing all my friends when I comes back to school after the holidays.

Ben

Write your own postcard

Now that you have perfected Ben's postcard, write your own postcard in your book, telling someone you know about an interesting place you have visited. Use at least five Standard English verb forms in your writing.

Noun or pronoun?

Rule

You can use a **pronoun** to take the place of a noun to avoid repeating it too much. For example, you can replace a name with a pronoun.

- *Billy went on the internet because **Billy** needed to find some information about penguins.*
- *Billy went on the internet because **he** needed to find some information about penguins.*

Examples of pronouns include:

I	you	he	she	it	we	they
me	him	her	us	them		

Possessive pronouns can be used instead of a noun with an apostrophe to show possession.

- *Alisha had to tidy **Alisha's room** before she could go to the park with **Alisha's friends**.*
- *Alisha had to tidy **her room** before she could go to the park with **her friends**.*

Examples of possessive pronouns include:

my	your	his	her	its	our	their

abc

pronoun: a word that can take the place of a noun, for example: *he, him, they, us*

possessive pronoun: a pronoun that can take the place of a noun with an apostrophe to show possession

noun: a word used to name a place, a person, a thing, or an idea, for example: *leg, Scotland, woman, sadness*.

possession: who or what owns something

    Pinpoint English Grammar and Punctuation Year 4/P5

Name ___________________________

Class ___________________________

Underline the pronouns

1 *Dan got a new phone but he dropped it and it stopped working.*

2 *His mum took it back to the shop to get it repaired.*

3 *The man in the shop told her that he could definitely repair it.*

4 *She asked him how long it would take.*

5 *He said it should be ready in a week or so.*

Match the sentence with nouns to the sentence with pronouns

1 *Jessica ate an apple.*   *She ate it.*

Jack ate two bananas.   *He ate them.*

2 *Rosie gave Robbie a birthday present.*   *She gave it to her.*

Robbie's mum gave Rosie a sandwich.   *She gave it to him.*

3 *Millie and Molly bought some sandwiches.*   *She bought it.*

Millie bought a drink.   *They bought them.*

4 *The police chased a burglar.*   *They chased him.*

The policeman chased some burglars.   *He chased them.*

Name _______________________

Class _______________________

— Replace the underlined words with pronouns —

1 *Lia and Tia love listening to music so <u>Lia and Tia</u> always play <u>music</u> at full volume!*

_______________________   _______________________

2 *Maisie's computer froze so <u>Maisie</u> turned <u>the computer</u> off and on again.*

_______________________   _______________________

3 *Majid and I always get lunch together because <u>Majid and I</u> like to chat while we eat <u>lunch</u>.*

_______________________   _______________________

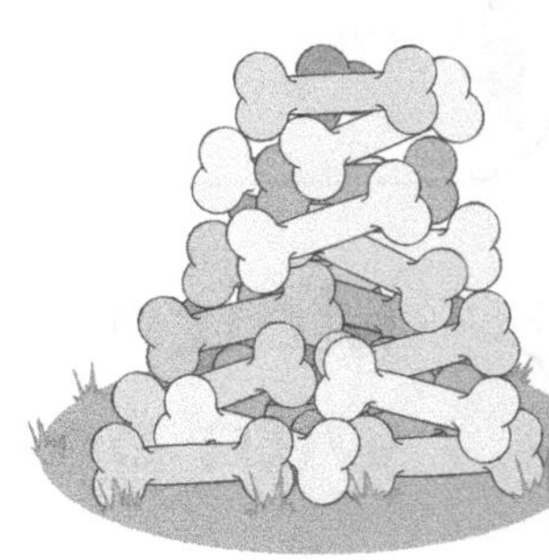

4 *Boris the dog loves bones but <u>Boris the dog</u> always forgets where <u>Boris the dog</u> has buried <u>the bones</u>.*

_______________________   _______________________

— Complete the sentence using pronouns —

1 *Grace bought some new shoes, but* _______________________

____.

2 *Harry tried spinach for the first time and he* _______________________.

3 *Mum and Dad said they would be back by 8 o'clock,*

but _______________________.

4 *Anita and I love playing rugby, but* _______________________

____.

You will need to use pronouns like *he, she, it, we, they, him* and *them*.

      Pinpoint English Grammar and Punctuation Year 4/P5

D **Name** ___________________________

Class ___________________________

Correct the pronouns

Matilda's restaurant review clearly shows her opinion, but lots of the nouns could be replaced with pronouns to make it sound better.

Cross out any nouns that could be replaced with pronouns.
Then add the correct pronouns.

Mario's Restaurant Review

I went with my family to Mario's, the new Italian restaurant in town last week. I am writing a review so that readers can decide if readers want to go and try Mario's.

I had spaghetti bolognese. The spaghetti bolognese was delicious. I ate all of the spaghetti bolognese! My sister had lasagne. She thought the lasagne was really nice and so was the salad she had with the lasagne. My parents both had meatballs. My parents said the meatballs were really good, and my parents really liked the pasta twirls that came with the meatballs.

The waiters were really nice and the waiters were really helpful. My family and I would all recommend this restaurant and my family and I will definitely be going back again.

Write your own review

Now that you have improved Matilda's review, write your own review in your book. It could be about your favourite book, film, or restaurant. Use at least five pronouns in your writing.

Rule

The following grammar and punctuation rules are covered in this revision unit.

1 In Standard English, verbs change depending on the person or the thing that is doing the action they describe.

I walk   *you walk*   *he walks*   *we walk*

I was walking   *you were walking*   *he was walking*   *we were walking*

2 You can use a pronoun to take the place of a noun so that you do not have to keep repeating it.

*Athletes must do a lot of training because **training** helps **athletes** improve.*

*Athletes must do a lot of training because **it** helps **them** improve.*

3 A possessive pronoun can take the place of a noun that has an apostrophe to show possession.

*The athlete prepared for **the athlete's** first big race.*

*The athlete prepared for **her** first big race.*

abc

pronoun: a word that can take the place of a noun, for example: *he, him, they, us*

possessive pronoun: a pronoun that can take the place of a noun with an apostrophe to show possession

      Pinpoint English Grammar and Punctuation Year 4/P5

Name _______________________

Class _______________________

Underline the non-Standard English verb forms

1 *We done really well in the test.*

2 *They done their homework two days before they had to hand it in.*

3 *We was running so fast it felt like flying!*

4 *I walks past the same dog on my way to school every day.*

5 *The food was all gone by the time they was at the front of the queue.*

Circle another way to write ...

1 *the rabbit ate the carrot.*

The rabbit ate it.   *The rabbit ate him.*   *The rabbit ate them.*

2 *Zak dropped the glasses.*

Zak dropped them.   *Zak dropped it.*   *Zak dropped his.*

3 *Leila ate the grapes.*

She ate them.   *She ate hers.*   *She ate they.*

4 *Anthony the cat ate Anthony the cat's breakfast.*

He ate his breakfast.   *It ate her breakfast.*   *She ate his breakfast.*

5 *Becca and Ethan went to Ethan's house.*

They went to their house.   *They went to his house.*

We went to his house.

S Name ______________________________

Class ______________________________

Correct the sentence to make it Standard English

1. *We was going on holiday.*

2. *Mum said I were taking ages to get my suitcase packed.*

3. *She weren't happy.*

4. *She kept asking, "Has you done it yet?"*

5. *"I has done it," I said eventually, and we was on our way.*

Rewrite the sentences using pronouns

1. *The leopard ran to a tree and climbed up the tree.*

   ____

2. *Mrs Clark was quite cross but Mrs Clark soon cheered up.*

   ____

3. *Jo and Josh baked some cupcakes but Jo and Josh did not eat the cupcakes.*

   ____

4. *Cinderella hated Cinderella's sisters because Cinderella's sisters were unkind to Cinderella.*

   ____

5. *My dad got on my dad's bike and my dad cycled into town.*

    Pinpoint English Grammar and Punctuation Year 4/P5

D **Name** ______________________

Class ______________________

Correct the verbs and pronouns

Dylan's recount gives lots of descriptive detail, but:

- some of the verb forms are not Standard English
- some of the nouns could be replaced with pronouns.

Circle all of the mistakes in one colour.
Then correct them in a second colour.

On Saturday, we was going for a walk in the woods with our dogs, Hattie and Maud. The sun were shining and there weren't a cloud in the sky. The dogs was very excited and the dogs was running about all over the place.

After a while, we stopped and had something to eat. Dad had brought some cheese and tomato sandwiches but the sandwiches was not very nice. I think the sandwiches had got squashed in dad's rucksack. The sandwiches looked like the sandwiches had been run over by a truck.

After lunch, we decided to throw the ball for the dogs. The dogs done plenty of barking when the dogs was chasing the ball! After that, the dogs was exhausted.

We was just deciding to go home, when …

Continue the story

Now that you have perfected the recount, continue the story of Dylan's day in your book. Try to write in Standard English and use at least three pronouns.

Expanding noun phrases

Rule

A noun phrase includes a noun and all the words that add information about it. The most important word in a noun phrase is the noun.

Noun phrases can be expanded to add detail or make them more interesting. You can do this in lots of different ways.

For example, you could add adjectives or use prepositions to build other phrases into the noun phrase.

house —————————— noun

the old house —————————— noun phrase expanded with an adjective

the old house with broken windows —————————— noun phrase expanded with adjectives and prepositions

story —————————— noun

an exciting story —————————— noun phrase expanded with an adjective

an exciting story about a flying spaceship —————————— noun phrase expanded with adjectives and prepositions

---

abc

noun: a word used to name a place, a person, a thing, or an idea, for example: *leg, Scotland, woman, sadness*

noun phrase: a group of words containing a noun and other words that add information about it, for example: *the tall boy with the dark hair*

preposition: a word that links a noun, pronoun or noun phrase to other words in the sentence, for example: *on, after, because of*

   Pinpoint English Grammar and Punctuation Year 4/P5

T **Name** ______________________________

Class ______________________________

Underline the noun phrase

1. *A little girl went walking.*

2. *A huge wolf suddenly appeared.*

3. *His dark green eyes stared at her.*

4. *He had huge, white teeth.*

5. *There was a small cottage with roses growing up the wall.*

Look for the noun and any other words or phrases that add information about the noun.

Match the answers to expand the noun phrase

1. *a hairy brown spider* *with a bushy beard*
   an elderly man *with eight spindly legs*

2. *some mouldy baked beans* *with a very loud cry*
   a small, sobbing baby *in a rusty can*

3. *a delicious fruit salad* *with oranges and apples*
   a splatter of my mud *on my face*

4. *a loud, screeching noise* *on his feet*
   a pair of shiny new trainers *in my ear*

Name _______________________________

Class _______________________________

Expand the noun phrases using these words

*tall   huge   small   tiny   red   black
pink   dark   shiny   beautiful   silent*

1 She lived in a _______________ house with a _______________ garden.

2 The _______________ tiger prowled through the _______________ shadows.

3 I found myself in a _______________ forest of _______________ trees.

4 A _______________ man with a _______________ nose drove up in a _______________ car.

Write your own sentence about ...

1 *a dinosaur.* Use an expanded noun phrase.

____

2 *a mouse.* Use an expanded noun phrase.

____

3 *a plate of food.* Use an expanded noun phrase.

____

4 *a hat.* Use an expanded noun phrase.

____

Use adjectives and prepositions (words like *in, on, with*) to add description to your noun phrase.

      Pinpoint English Grammar and Punctuation Year 4/P5

D **Name** _______________________________

Class _______________________________

Expand the noun phrases

This advert gives some information, but it could be much more descriptive if it used expanded noun phrases.

Circle all the nouns that could be expanded.
Then think of some words and phrases to expand the noun phrases and add them in the right places.

Palace For Sale

As you walk through the palace's gates, you will see the palace gardens. They are full of flowers and trees. When you enter the palace, you will find yourself in the main hall. The floor is made of marble and the walls are decorated with tapestries. At the end of the hall is a throne.

As you leave the main hall, you enter the banqueting room where there is a table for you and your guests to enjoy meals, created by the palace chef. The banqueting hall is lit with chandeliers and decorated with suits of armour.

A stairway from the banqueting room leads to the palace's twenty-four bedrooms. Each one has its own bathroom, featuring a bath with taps.

Also included: 150 servants.

Write your own advert

Now that you have added detail to the advert, write your own advert in your book. Use at least three expanded noun phrases in your writing.

Rule

An adverbial adds information to a verb. You can use adverbials to add information about time, place or the way in which something is done.

An adverbial can be a word.

- *I **suddenly** realised I was late.*

It can also be a phrase.

- *I ran all the way to school **as quickly as I could**.*

If you put an adverbial at the start of a sentence, it is called a fronted adverbial. It is always separated from the rest of the sentence by a comma.

- ***Suddenly,*** *I realised I was late.*
- ***As quickly as I could,*** *I ran all the way to school.*

adverbial: a word or group of words that acts as an adverb describing how, where or when something happened

fronted adverbial: a group of words at the start of a sentence that shows how, where or when something is happening

          Pinpoint English Grammar and Punctuation Year 4/P5

Name ______________________

Class ______________________

Underline the adverbial

1. *I was hurriedly getting ready to meet my friends.*

2. *I was supposed to meet my friends at six o'clock.*

3. *I waited outside the cinema.*

4. *My friends arrived eventually.*

5. *The film was going to start in two minutes.*

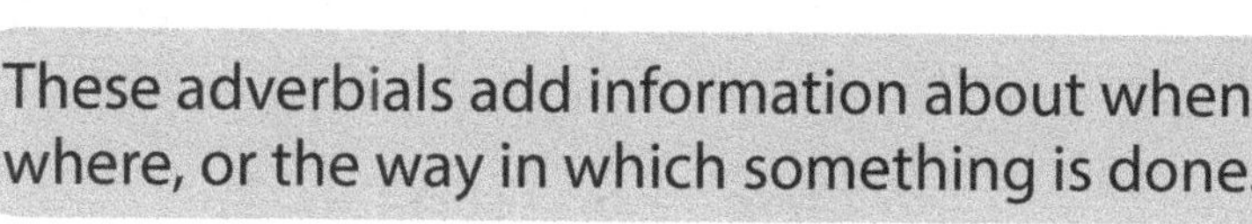

Tick the sentences that use fronted adverbials

1. *After several years in Australia, my aunt and uncle moved back to London.*

2. *Nobody knows if there is life on other planets.*

3. *Holding my breath, I dived into the water.*

4. *Early the next morning, I was woken by a loud crash.*

5. *I opened my presents with trembling fingers.*

     Pinpoint English Grammar and Punctuation Year 4/P5   **35**

Name _______________________

Class _______________________

Complete the sentence using a fronted adverbial

Last week   *With their hands in the air*   *At half-time*
Seconds later   *Within a few minutes*

1 ___________________ *the boys and the girls played football.*

2 ___________________ *the boys scored the first goal.*

3 ___________________ *the girls scored a goal, and then another goal.*

4 ___________________ *the girls celebrated excitedly.*

5 ___________________ *the score was 3–3.*

Write your own sentence about ...

1 *a place you have visited recently.* Use an adverbial.

____

2 *something you would like to do in the future.* Use a fronted adverbial.

____

3 *an object that is somewhere in your home.* Use an adverbial.

____

4 *a place that is near your home.* Use a fronted adverbial.

____

5 *what you were doing at seven o'clock last night.* Use an adverbial.

____

     Pinpoint English Grammar and Punctuation Year 4/P5

D **Name** ______________________________

Class ______________________________

Add some adverbials

This headteacher's letter gives lots of information about the improvements she is planning for her school but it needs some adverbials to give more information about when and where these improvements will be made.

Circle all of the places where adverbials or fronted adverbials could be added. Then add some adverbials and fronted adverbials.

Dear Parents and Carers,

We are planning some exciting improvements.

Lockers will be fitted so that students can safely store their belongings.

We are going to redecorate Year 3 and Year 4's classrooms.

We will be building a new music and drama studio.

We will be providing every classroom with new laptops and tablets to support our students' learning.

If you would like any more information about these improvements, do please contact me.

Yours faithfully,

Ms E Tallah

Headteacher

Write your own review

Now that you have improved the headteacher's letter, write a letter to your headteacher, suggesting some improvements that you would like to be made in your school. Use at least three fronted adverbials in your writing.

Rule

The following grammar and punctuation rules are covered in this revision unit.

1 You can expand noun phrases by adding extra detail. For example, you can add adjectives.

an apple ⟶ *a **crunchy** apple* ⟶ *a **delicious, crunchy** apple*

2 You can expand noun phrases even more by using prepositions to build in other phrases.

*A delicious, crunchy apple **in my lunchbox**.*

*A delicious, crunchy apple **in my green lunchbox with dinosaurs on it**.*

3 Adverbials can add information to verbs about about the time, place or way in which something is done. They can be words or phrases.

*The apple **mysteriously** disappeared **after lunch**.*

4 A fronted adverbial comes at the start of a sentence and is separated from the rest of the sentence by a comma.

***After lunch,** the apple **mysteriously** disappeared.*

abc

adverbial: a word or group of words that acts as an adverb describing how, where or when something happened

fronted adverbial: a group of words at the start of a sentence that shows how, where or when something is happening

preposition: a word that links a noun, pronoun or noun phrase to other words in the sentence, for example: *on, after, because of*

  Pinpoint English Grammar and Punctuation Year 4/P5

Name ______________________

Class ______________________

Tick the sentences that use an expanded noun phrase

1 *A mighty wind howled and towering waves crashed over the tiny ship.*

2 *Sailors ran about on deck, helplessly trying to shield themselves.*

3 *The ancient timbers of the ship creaked and groaned.*

4 *Nobody knew if they would survive.*

5 *Tall, ragged cliffs loomed in the distance.*

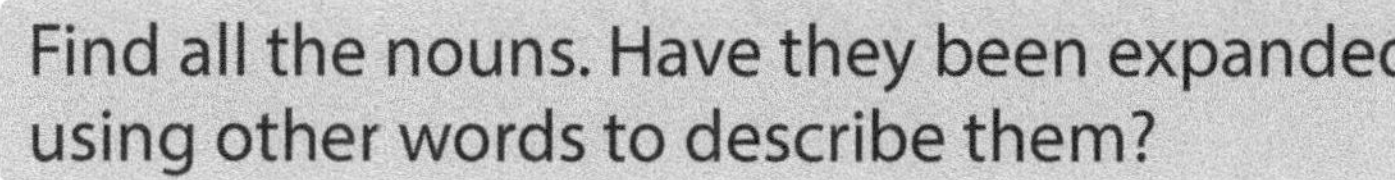

Underline the fronted adverbials

1 *Before the test, Naz felt very nervous.*

2 *After the test, Naz felt much better.*

3 *On his farm, the farmer kept a thousand sheep.*

4 *In his barn, the farmer kept his chickens.*

5 *On the sailor's shoulder, sat a monkey.*

Name ______________________

Class ______________________

Replace the underlined noun with an expanded noun phrase

1 *Raz put on his <u>trainers</u> and headed for the front door.*

____

2 *A <u>dragon</u> flew overhead.*

____

3 *Rapunzel let down her <u>hair</u>.*

____

4 *Scuttling towards me, was a <u>rat</u>.*

____

You could add an adjective or a phrase beginning with a preposition to expand the noun phrase.

Complete the sentence using a fronted adverbial

1 ______________, *we set off on a long cycle ride through the countryside.*

2 ______________, *we sat down for a picnic.*

3 ______________, *we took a wrong turn.*

4 ______________, *we realised we had no idea where we were.*

5 ______________, *we found our way home.*

Fronted adverbials could say when or where these things happened.

    Pinpoint English Grammar and Punctuation Year 4/P5

D **Name** _______________________

Class _______________________

Expand the noun phrases and add adverbials

This story uses some description and detail, but it could be even better if it used expanded noun phrases and adverbials.

Add some adverbials and expanded noun phrases to the story to create more detail.

The Lamp

"I'm home!" called Dad. "And I have found treasures!"

My dad had been to the car boot sale. I was trying to watch television. He came into the room and dumped a box full of rubbish. He started taking things out of the box and spreading them out. There were dolls, toys, books and a lamp.

Dad went to tell Mum about the treasure he had brought home. I could hear Mum groaning and I laughed.

I found myself picking up the lamp. It had some markings on it. I began to rub the lamp and, to my amazement …

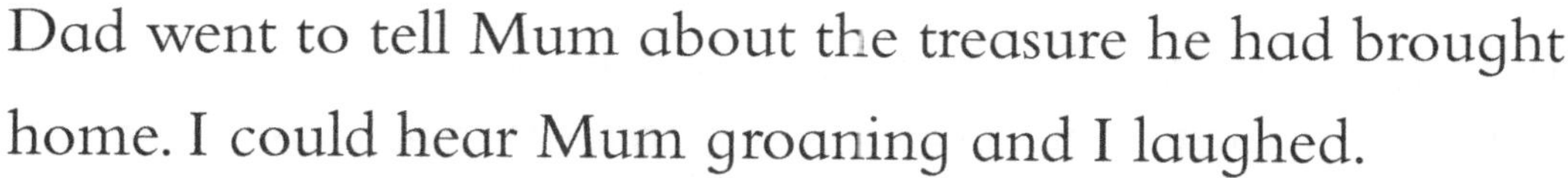

Continue the story

Now that you have added more detail the beginning of the story, continue it in your book. Use at least three expanded noun phrases and three adverbials in your writing.

Rule

A paragraph is a group of sentences that are linked in some way. It might be because:

- they are about the same topic
- they are about the same person
- they are about events that are happening at the same time.

The sentences in this first paragraph below are **about recycling**.

More than half of the rubbish we make can be recycled. For example, all the tin cans we throw away can be made into something new. Recycling one tin can save enough energy to run a television for three hours.

The sentences in the second paragraph are **about using less energy**. This is a different topic so they are put in a new paragraph.

Recycling is not the only way in which we can be kind to the environment. Another way is to use less electricity and gas – by switching off lights when we leave a room, for example. Using less energy means less pollution.

When you start a new paragraph, you can start a new line and indent it. Or, you can leave an empty line between paragraphs.

abc

paragraph: a group of sentences that are linked by topic, time or place

indent: leaving a space on the line before you write the first word

   Pinpoint English Grammar and Punctuation Year 4/P5

T **Name** ______________________________

Class ______________________________

Tick the sentences that go in the same paragraph

1 *A bee flaps its wings about two hundred times every second.*

2 *This makes a buzzing sound as it flies.*

3 *Bees fly from flower to flower, collecting the nectar which they will make into honey.*

4 *Wasps also make a buzzing sound, but they do not make honey.*

Tick one box to mark a new paragraph

1 *"What are you doing for sports day?" asked Max.* ☐ *"The egg and spoon race," said Alice.* ☐ *"I'm a champion egg and spoon racer," she added.* ☐ *"The others won't stand a chance!"*

2 *Venus is the nearest planet to ours.* ☐ *It is about the same size as Earth but the temperature on Venus is hot enough to melt lead!* ☐ *Mars is smaller than Earth.* ☐ *Some scientists believe there may be some forms of life on this small, red planet.* ☐

3 *Ellie and I are going to visit Auntie Jan and Uncle Steve next week.* ☐ *We're really looking forward to seeing them and all the dogs and cats!* ☐ *Ellie will be starting her new school in September.* ☐ *I think she is quite excited about it.*

Name _______________________

Class _______________________

Sort these sentences into paragraphs I and 2

I *Many people think that homework is an important part of children's learning.*

paragraph _______________

2 *However, other people believe that too much homework is a problem.*

paragraph _______________

3 *They believe homework gives children an opportunity to practise their skills at home.*

paragraph _______________

4 *They also think that homework gives students the chance to learn by themselves.*

paragraph _______________

5 *They say that children who spend all their time doing homework have no time left to enjoy themselves.*

paragraph _______________

Write a short paragraph about ...

I *your favourite book.*

____

____

2 *your favourite film.*

____

____

    Pinpoint English Grammar and Punctuation Year 4/P5

D Name ______________________

Class ______________________

Correct the paragraphing

This report is full of information, but it is not written in paragraphs.

Correct the paragraphing in these sentences by marking where each new paragraph should begin.
Mark the beginning of each paragraph with a double slash (//).

Animation

When you watch an animated film, twenty four pictures flash in front of your eyes every second and make you think the pictures are moving. It took a quarter of a million different drawings to make the very first full length animation film. Most animated films are now made using computers. This works in the same way as older films, but the pictures are not drawn by hand. Computers can do some of the work, but animators still have to tell them what to do! One other kind of animation is called stop-motion. This is where a picture is taken of a real object. The object is then moved slightly and another picture is taken. The animator has to do this twenty-four times just to make one second of film.

Write your own report

Now that you have perfected the paragraphing in the report, write your own report in your book. Write at least three paragraphs.

Rule

When we punctuate direct speech, we put the words that are spoken inside inverted commas or speech marks.

- *"I wonder what could be inside the box."*

There is always a punctuation mark at the end of the spoken words, before the closing speech marks.

Sometimes we add a reporting clause to speech. This tells the reader who is speaking.

- **Pandora said,** *"I wonder what could be inside the box."*

There is always a punctuation mark at the end of the reporting clause. If the reporting clause comes before the speech, there is a comma at the end of it.

If the reporting clause is the end of the sentence, there is a full stop at the end of it.

- *"I wonder what could be inside the box,"* **said Pandora.**

---

abc

inverted commas: punctuation marks used to show direct speech (sometimes called speech marks)

reporting clause: the words that tell the reader who is speaking, for example: *he said* or *said Alice*

    Pinpoint English Grammar and Punctuation Year 4/P5

Name ___________________________

Class ___________________________

Tick the sentences that use speech punctuation correctly

1. *"Knock knock, said Naveed.*

2. *Sam asked, "Who's there?"*

3. *"Boo" replied Naveed.*

4. *Sam asked "Boo who?"*

5. *"Don't cry! It's only a joke," said Naveed.*

Add one comma and one full stop

1. *"My shoes need to be cleaned* ☐ *"* ☐ *said Griselda* ☐

2. *Cindy replied* ☐ *"But I haven't finished washing your socks yet* ☐ *"* ☐

3. *"Then you must wash them more quickly* ☐ *"* ☐ *shrieked Griselda* ☐

4. *Cindy muttered* ☐ *"All these stinky socks will take hours to wash* ☐ *"* ☐

5. *"And your shoes smell even worse than your socks* ☐ *"* ☐ *she added* ☐

S **Name** _______________________

Class _______________________

Complete the sentence using a reporting clause

1 "I have created an amazing new

invention _________________ .

2 "What is it _________________ .

3 "It's a flying robot _________________ .

4 "That's amazing! How does it fly _________________ .

5 "I'm not sure yet _________________ .

> Check your punctuation very carefully! You will need to use speech marks, commas, full stops and question marks.

Correct the punctuation

1 Someone has been eating my porridge said Baby Bear

2 Priti asked Alfie Can I borrow your colouring pencils

3 It's a secret whispered Jacob

4 I'm going to make a cake said Joe

5 Katie yelled Oh no, I dropped the eggs

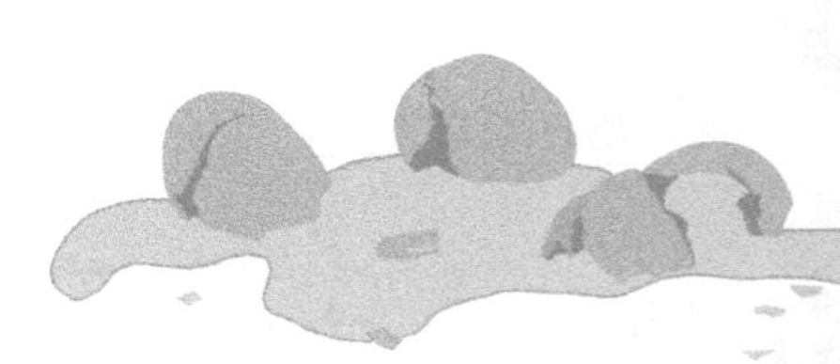

      Pinpoint English Grammar and Punctuation Year 4/P5

D **Name** ______________________

Class ______________________

Correct the speech punctuation

This story is mysterious and gripping but some of its speech punctuation is missing.

Underline all of the words that are spoken by the characters in one colour. Then add the correct speech punctuation in a second colour.

The Secret Door

Cara knocked on the front door and waited. When her grandmother opened the door, Cara threw herself through it and gave her granny a big hug.

Hello, Granny said Cara.

Hello, my dear said Granny.

I've been looking forward to staying with you for ages said Cara grinning broadly and sitting down in the front room.

Granny smiled and said Me too. I've got a surprise for you. Come with me.

Granny went out into the hallway. She stood looking down at the floor. There was a little wooden door in the floorboards.

What is it, Granny she asked.

Granny smiled, bent down and lifted open the little door …

Continue the story

Now that you have corrected the beginning of the story, continue it in your book. Use at least three correctly-punctuated pieces of speech in your writing.

Rule

The following grammar and punctuation rules are covered in this revision unit.

 **1** You should start a new paragraph when:

- you change topic
- you write about a different person
- a different person starts speaking
- the events in the paragraph are happening at a different time.

When you start a new paragraph, you can start a new line and indent your writing, or leave a blank line.

Jack came over the hill, puffing and sweating. His face was very red. He was carrying two empty buckets.

"Hi," said Jill.

"Hello," said Jack. "We need to get some water."

 **2** When you write direct speech, you should:

- put the words that are spoken inside inverted commas or speech marks
- add a punctuation mark at the end of the spoken words, before the closing speech marks
- add a punctuation mark at the end of the reporting clause (if you have used one).

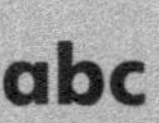 **indent**: leaving a space on the line before you write the first word

inverted commas: punctuation marks used to show direct speech (sometimes called speech marks)

reporting clause: the words that tell the reader who is speaking, for example: *he said* or *said Alice*

     Pinpoint English Grammar and Punctuation Year 4/P5

T **Name** _______________

Class _______________

Tick one box to mark a new paragraph

1 During the stone age, most humans lived as hunter-gatherers. ☐ This means they did not grow their own food. ☐ They had to go and hunt for meat and gather wild plants. ☐ Stone age people lived in caves.

2 The king said to Hercules, "You must beat the Hydra. That is your first task." ☐ "How should I beat it?" asked Hercules, feeling nervous. ☐ He waited for the king to reply. ☐ It felt like a very long time.

3 The school concert was a great success. ☐ It was a complete sellout! ☐ Sports day was another highlight of the year. ☐ Every student took part and we all enjoyed the excellent weather.

Circle the correct use of speech punctuation

1 Dee said "You're late."   Dee said, "You're late"
Dee said, "You're late."

2 "I'm starving!" said Bea.   "I'm starving" said Bea.
I'm starving! said Bea.

3 "Who's there" yelled Mani.   "Who's there?" yelled Mani.
"Who's there?" yelled Mani

4 Ivy said, Thanks!   Ivy said "Thanks!"
Ivy said, "Thanks!"

S Name ___________________

Class ___________________

Add a double slash (//) to show where you would start a new paragraph

Since the internet became widely available just thirty years ago, it has grown and grown.   Now we can access millions of words and images about millions of topics, without leaving our homes.   The internet is an amazing source of information and entertainment.   Simply by typing two or three words into a search engine, you can find exactly what we need.   It could be an online shop, an online encyclopaedia, or an online game!   One of the most popular uses of the internet is to keep in touch with family and friends.   You can use the internet to send a message to your next-door neighbours, or a message to your relatives on the other side of the world.   Because the words are sent electronically, they take less than a second to arrive!

Look out for changes in topic. There are three paragraphs altogether, so you need to mark // two times.

Use direct speech and speech punctuation to rewrite …

1 *Amber asked if she could have another sandwich.*

____

2 *Chloe's dad asked her what she would like for dinner.*

____

3 *Zack said sorry to Mrs Bromley.*

____

4 *Julius Caesar says he will invade England.*

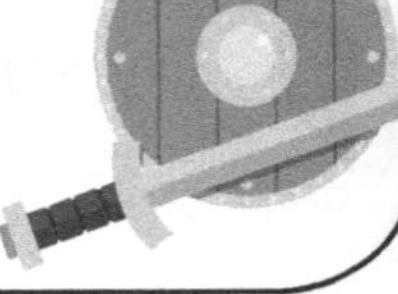

____

        Pinpoint English Grammar and Punctuation Year 4/P5

D **Name** ______________________

Class ______________________

Add paragraphs and speech punctuation

Temi's diary entry is full of interesting detail but she has forgotten to write in paragraphs or to use speech punctuation.

Mark where each paragraph should begin by adding a double slash (//) in one colour.
Then, add speech punctuation in a second colour.

<u>19th April</u>

We went to Farm Fun today. It is a farm where you can see all the animals and feed them. You can also go on a rowing boat on the lake, play in the Adventure Barn and even ride on a tractor! My favourite animals were the sheep because they had lambs. They were running round all over the place, clambering over each other and bleating. On the way home, Mum asked Do you want to be a sheep farmer when you're older? Maybe I said. I have now decided that I am going to be a vet when I grow up. I think it would be amazing to save animals' lives. I think I might be a vet for pets though. Cows, horses and sheep are quite big. I think I would rather help dogs and cats and hamsters!

Continue the story

Now that you have perfected Temi's diary, write your own diary entry about a day in your life. Try to:

- write at least three paragraphs
- include at least two correctly punctuated pieces of direct speech.

Answers

Page 7

Activity 1

1 The spider's <u>webs</u> stretched across the <u>blades</u> of grass.
2 The <u>raindrops</u> raced down the house's <u>windows</u>.
3 The castle's <u>walls</u> are twenty <u>metres</u> tall.
4 The <u>dogs</u> have chewed the table's <u>legs</u>.
5 The cat's <u>whiskers</u> twitched.

> There is only one cat but it has lots of whiskers!

Activity 2

1 There were strange noises coming from our <u>car's</u> engine.
2 A <u>lion's</u> roar can be heard from a distance of five miles.
3 My <u>mum's</u> earrings are made of coloured beads.
4 The <u>tree's</u> leaves fly through the air on windy autumn days.
5 The <u>dog's</u> muddy paw prints went all the way up the stairs.

> The engine belongs to the car. All the other words that end in *s* in this sentence are plurals.

Page 8

Activity 1

1 <u>Amy's</u> <u>shoes</u> were much too small for her feet.
2 Some of <u>Britain's</u> <u>rivers</u> are very polluted with plastic.
3 The <u>tyres</u> on Millie's bicycle are flat.
4 My sister's <u>friends</u> are all going to <u>Adil's</u> party.
5 My <u>school's</u> <u>computers</u> were going very slowly in today's lessons.

> The apostrophes are correct in the words *Millie's* and *sister's*.

Activity 2

1 the rabbit's ears
2 the football player's boots
3 the teacher's car
4 Our neighbour's garden is much tidier than our garden.
5 There was a smile on the girl's face when her team won.

> Check you haven't added an apostrophe to any plurals that do not need one.

Page 9

Activity 1

> The feathers belong to the raven.

… shiny as a <u>raven's</u> feathers. Both had dark <u>eyes</u> …
… flowing down their <u>backs</u>, almost reaching their waists.
… shriek and scream at the top of their <u>voices</u>.
It always brought a smile to their <u>mum's</u> face.
… complete silence when the <u>twins</u> were in their bedroom.
This filled their <u>mum's</u> mind with worrying <u>thoughts</u>.
… They would wear each <u>other's</u> clothes …
… Their <u>tricks</u> never fooled their mother though …

> *Backs* and *eyes* are plurals, not possessives, so they don't need apostrophes.

Activity 2

Use this checklist to mark your answer.
My description …

☐ … uses interesting language

☐ … makes a clear picture of the character

☐ … correctly uses at least three plurals

☐ … correctly uses at least three possessive apostrophes.

Answers

Page II

Activity I

I the beady eyes belonging to the eagles → the eagles' beady eyes
   the beady eyes belonging to the eagle → the eagle's beady eyes
2 the long ears belonging to the donkey → the donkey's long ears
   the long ears belonging to the donkeys → the donkeys' long ears
3 the sharp claws belonging to the tiger → the tiger's sharp claws
   the sharp claws belonging to the tigers → the tigers' sharp claws
4 the hairy legs belonging to the spiders → the spiders' hairy legs
   the hairy legs belonging to the spider → the spider's hairy legs

Activity 2

I the birds' singing
2 the flowers' smell
3 the dogs' barking
4 people's lives

> Remember, for plurals that end in *s* you just add an apostrophe.

Page I2

Activity I

I The <u>children's</u> packed lunches were delicious and very healthy.
2 Four hungry <u>horses'</u> heads peered at me over the top of the <u>bushes</u>.
3 I spilt a glass of water on both my <u>parents' phones</u>.
4 Some <u>women's</u> hats blew away in the high <u>winds</u>.
5 The <u>buses' wheels</u> went round and round.

> The plural of *bus* is *buses*.

Activity 2

For example:
I The air was filled with the lorries' smelly fumes.
2 The children's scooters were kept in the garden.
3 The cats' toys were scattered all over the house.
4 The tree's leaves rustled in the breeze.

Page I3

Activity I

… The school wants to improve the <u>students'</u> health …
… that she gathered all the <u>teachers'</u> opinions …
… "All the <u>teachers</u> agree that chocolate is bad for the <u>children's</u> teeth and bad for the <u>children's</u> health," …
… Some of the <u>students'</u> parents are very happy …
… what goes in our <u>children's</u> packed lunches …
… the school should listen to the <u>parents'</u> opinions …

> Watch out for the irregular plural *children*.

Activity 2

Use this checklist to mark your answer.
My newspaper article …

☐ … has a headline
☐ … uses formal language
☐ … contains facts
☐ … correctly uses at least three possessive apostrophes with plural nouns.

Page 15

Activity 1

1 women
2 mice
3 the women's clothes
4 the mouse's cheese
5 the people's voices

> *Women* and *people* are irregular plurals that do not end in *s*, so you need to add 's to show possession.

Activity 2

1 It was <u>Mel's</u> first day at her new school so her stomach was full of butterflies and her palms were sweating.
2 As she watched her <u>parents'</u> car disappear into the distance, she felt tears welling up in her eyes.
3 Mel saw huge crowds of boys and girls, but she did not know <u>anybody's</u> name.
4 Then she saw two <u>girls'</u> faces smiling at her and all her feelings of fear were gone.

Page 16

Activity 1

1 The <u>girls</u> set off for the park on their <u>skateboards</u>.
2 Their <u>skateboards'</u> wheels clattered over the pavement.
3 The <u>girls'</u> chattering voices could be heard for miles around.
4 Suddenly, one <u>girl's</u> skateboard skidded to a halt.
5 One of her <u>skateboard's</u> wheels had come off!

> First you need to work out how many girls and how many skateboards the sentence is about. Then think about where an apostrophe should go.

Activity 2

1 <u>The sun's rays</u> shone through <u>the trees' leaves</u>.
2 The ball flew off <u>Mari's boot</u> and sailed into <u>the other team's goal</u>.
3 <u>The fire's flames</u> warmed <u>Tom's frozen toes</u>.
4 <u>The flower's petals</u> slowly opened one bright <u>summer's day</u>.

Page 17

Activity 1

The <u>Magician's</u> House
The <u>house's</u> walls were made of grey stone.
… smoke rose from the <u>house's</u> tall chimney …
… hovered in the air like tufts of <u>sheep's</u> wool.
… they heard <u>someone's</u> footsteps approaching. The <u>door's</u> hinges creaked …
… "Good morning," said one of the <u>man's</u> parrots.
… The <u>children's</u> eyes widened in surprise. The two <u>parrots'</u> four beady eyes …

> Well done if you spotted this tricky apostrophe!

Activity 2

Use this checklist to mark your answer.
My story …

☐ … explains what happens next
☐ … correctly uses at least three apostrophes of possession.
☐ … captures the reader's imagination

   Pinpoint English Grammar and Punctuation Year 4/P5

Page 19

Activity 1

1 We were late. → Standard English
   We was late. → non-Standard English
2 You was early. → non-Standard English
   You were early. → Standard English
3 They was running. → non-Standard English
   They were running. → Standard English
4 He was walking quickly. → Standard English
   He were walking quickly. → non-Standard English
5 I was walking quickly. → Standard English
   I were walking quickly. → non-standard English

You might use non-standard English when you are talking to people you know well, but it is important to be able to use standard English in your writing.

Activity 2

1 I go out.
2 She goes in.
3 We say sorry.
4 We have done it.
5 He was busy.

Page 20

Activity 1

1 We went to the cinema and watched a film which <u>was</u> really good.
2 After the film, we <u>were</u> hungry so we went for a pizza.
3 We did not order a dessert because we <u>were</u> completely full!
4 Then my little sister started crying because she <u>was</u> so tired.
5 I <u>said</u> to my mum, "We should have left her at home!"

To be is a tricky but very common irregular verb. Make sure you learn it.

Activity 2

1 I was so happy reading my book!
2 The sun was shining.
3 There wasn't a cloud in the sky.
4 The birds were singing in the trees.

Page 21

Activity 1

… We <u>are</u> having an amazing time in London.
We <u>have</u> been to the Tower of London, which <u>was</u> interesting …
… London Eye which <u>was</u> really exciting. When you <u>are</u> at the top …
… you <u>see</u> the whole of London and all the people below <u>look</u> like tiny ants!
Tomorrow we <u>go</u> to the London Dungeon. My brother <u>has</u> been before and he <u>says</u>
it <u>is</u> scary. I <u>hope</u> I <u>am</u> brave and <u>do</u> not start screaming.
I <u>am</u> looking forward to seeing my friends when I <u>come</u> back to school …

Ben is writing to his teacher, so he needs to use formal standard English.

Activity 2

Use this checklist to mark your answer.
My postcard …

☐ … describes the place you visited

☐ … explains what you did there

☐ … correctly uses at least five
    Standard English verb forms.

Page 23

Activity 1

1 Dan got a new phone but <u>he</u> dropped <u>it</u> and <u>it</u> stopped working.
2 <u>His</u> mum took <u>it</u> back to the shop to get <u>it</u> repaired.
3 The man in the shop told <u>her</u> that <u>he</u> could definitely repair <u>it</u>.
4 <u>She</u> asked <u>him</u> how long <u>it</u> would take.
5 <u>He</u> said <u>it</u> should be ready in a week or so.

> Look out for all the pronouns that have taken the place of Dan, the phone, Dan's mum and the man in the shop.

Activity 2

1 Jessica ate an apple. → She ate it.
  Jack ate two bananas. → He ate them.
2 Rosie gave Robbie a birthday present. → She gave it to him.
  Robbie's mum gave Rosie a sandwich. → She gave it to her.
3 Millie and Molly bought some sandwiches. → They bought them.
  Millie bought a drink. → She bought it.
4 The police chased a burglar. → They chased him.
  The policeman chased some burglars. → He chased them.

Page 24

Activity 1

1 Lia and Tia love listening to music so <u>they</u> always play <u>it</u> at top volume!
2 Maisie's computer froze so <u>she</u> turned <u>it</u> off and on again.
3 Majid and I always get lunch together because <u>we</u> like to chat while we eat <u>it</u>.
4 Boris the dog loves bones but <u>he</u> always forgets where <u>he</u> has buried <u>them</u>.

Activity 2

For example:
1 Grace bought some new shoes but <u>they were too small.</u>
2 Harry tried spinach for the first time and he <u>loved it</u>.
3 Mum and Dad said they would be back by 8 o'clock, but <u>they were late</u>.
4 Megan and I love playing rugby, but <u>we prefer basketball</u>.

> Try underlining all the nouns in the sentence to help you decide which ones could be replaced with pronouns.

Page 25

Activity 1

… writing a review so that <u>you</u> can decide if <u>you</u> want to go and try <u>it</u>.
… <u>It</u> was delicious. I ate all of <u>it</u>!
… She thought <u>it</u> was really nice …
… the salad she had with <u>it</u>.
… <u>They</u> said the meatballs were really good, and <u>they</u> really liked the pasta twirls that came with <u>them</u>.
… really nice and <u>they</u> were really helpful.
… <u>we</u> will definitely be going back again.

> You can change the word *readers* to *you* because you are talking directly to the reader.

Activity 2

Use this checklist to mark your answer.
My review …

☐ … describes the book, film or restaurant
☐ … uses entertaining language
☐ … gives your opinion
☐ … correctly uses at least five pronouns.

    Pinpoint English Grammar and Punctuation Year 4/P5

Page 27

Activity 1

1 We <u>done</u> really well in the test.
2 They <u>done</u> their homework two days before they had to hand it in.
3 We <u>was</u> running so fast it felt like flying!
4 I <u>walks</u> past the same dog on my way to school every day.
5 The food was all gone by the time they <u>was</u> at the front of the queue.

Activity 2

1 The rabbit ate it.
2 Zak dropped them.
3 She ate them.
4 He ate his breakfast.
5 They went to his house.

Page 28

Activity 1

1 We <u>were</u> going on holiday.
2 Mum said I <u>was</u> taking ages to get my suitcase packed.
3 She <u>wasn't</u> happy.
4 She kept asking, "<u>Have</u> you done it yet?"
5 "I <u>have</u> done it," I said eventually, and we <u>were</u> on our way.

It's easy to get were and *was*, *have* and *has* mixed up!

Activity 2

1 The leopard ran to a tree and climbed up <u>it</u>.
2 Mrs Clark was quite cross but <u>she</u> soon cheered up.
3 Jo and Josh baked some cupcakes but <u>they</u> did not eat <u>them</u>.
4 Cinderella hated <u>her</u> sisters because <u>they</u> were unkind to <u>her</u>.
5 My dad got on <u>his</u> bike and <u>he</u> cycled into town

Page 29

Activity 1

On Saturday, we <u>were</u> going for a walk …
… The sun <u>was</u> shining and there <u>wasn't</u> a cloud …
… The dogs <u>were</u> very excited and <u>they</u> <u>were</u> running about all over the place.
… but <u>they</u> <u>were</u> not very nice. I think <u>they</u> had got squashed …
… <u>They</u> looked like <u>they</u> had been run over by a truck.
… <u>They</u> <u>did</u> plenty of barking when <u>they</u> <u>were</u> chasing the ball!
After that, <u>they</u> <u>were</u> exhausted.
We <u>were</u> just deciding to go home, when …

Did you spot the possessive pronouns *her* and *his*?

Activity 2

Use this checklist to mark your answer.
My recount …

There were lots of corrections to make in Dylan's recount. Well done if you spotted most of them!

☐ … is in chronological order

☐ … correctly uses Standard English

☐ … explains what happens next

☐ … correctly uses at least three pronouns.

Page 31

Activity 1

1 <u>A little girl</u> went walking.
2 <u>A huge wolf</u> suddenly appeared.
3 <u>His dark green eyes</u> stared at her.
4 He had <u>huge, white teeth</u>.
5 There was <u>a small cottage with roses growing up the wall</u>.

> Make sure you have underlined the whole noun phrase.

Activity 2

1 a hairy brown spider → with eight spindly legs
   an elderly man → with a bushy beard
2 some mouldy baked beans → in a rusty can
   a small, sobbing baby → with a very loud cry
3 a delicious fruit salad → with oranges and apples
   a splatter of my mud → on my face
4 a loud, screeching noise → in my ear
   a pair of shiny new trainers → on his feet

Page 32

Activity 1

For example:
1 She lived in a <u>tiny</u> house with a <u>beautiful</u> garden.
2 The <u>silent</u> tiger prowled through the <u>black</u> shadows.
3 I found myself in a <u>dark</u> forest of <u>tall</u> trees.
4 A <u>small</u> man with a <u>huge pink</u> nose drove up in a <u>shiny red</u> car.

> Choose your words carefully. Making a noun phrase longer does not always make it better!

Activity 2

For example:
1 A ferocious dinosaur with sharp yellow teeth leapt from behind the trees.
2 A little grey mouse with twitching whiskers scurried across the floor.
3 I had a slice of pizza with a crisp, green salad.
4 My grandma wore a tall, green hat with feathers on the top.

Page 33

Activity 1

For example:
… the palace's <u>strong, iron</u> gates … the <u>impressive</u> palace gardens.
… full of <u>colourful</u> flowers and <u>beautiful</u> trees.
… you will find yourself in the <u>magnificent</u> main hall.
… made of <u>shiny, white</u> marble and the walls are decorated with <u>intricate</u> tapestries.
At the end of the hall is a <u>vast, jewel-encrusted</u> throne … there is a <u>long, wooden</u> table …
… enjoy <u>delicious</u> meals, created by the <u>talented</u> palace chef.
… lit with <u>sparkling</u> chandeliers and decorated with <u>shining silver</u> suits of armour.
A <u>wide</u> stairway from the banqueting room leads to the palace's twenty-four <u>amazing</u> bedrooms. … its own <u>luxurious</u> bathroom featuring a <u>deep</u> bath with <u>golden</u> taps.
Also included: 150 <u>loyal and obedient</u> servants.

Activity 2

Use this checklist to mark your answer.
My advert …

☐   … persuades the reader   ☐   … explains what is on offer

☐   … correctly uses at least three expanded noun phrases.

Answers

Page 35

Activity 1

1 I was <u>hurriedly</u> getting ready to meet my friends.
2 I was supposed to meet my friends <u>at six o'clock</u>.
3 I waited <u>outside the cinema</u>.
4 My friends arrived <u>eventually</u>.
5 The film was going to start <u>in two minutes</u>.

> In sentence 5, *with trembling fingers* is an adverbial, but it is not fronted.

Activity 2

1 After several years in Australia, my aunt and uncle moved back to London. ✔
3 Holding my breath, I dived into the water. ✔
4 Early the next morning, I was woken by a loud crash. ✔

Page 36

Activity 1

1 <u>Last week,</u> the boys and the girls played football.
2 <u>Within a few minutes,</u> the boys scored the first goal.
3 <u>Seconds later,</u> the girls scored a goal, and then another goal.
4 <u>With their hands in the air,</u> the girls celebrated excitedly.
5 <u>At half-time,</u> the score was 3–3.

> Check that you have separated each fronted adverbial from the rest of the sentence with a comma.

Activity 2

For example:

1 I went to the park <u>at the weekend</u>.
2 <u>In the next two years,</u> I want to get my black belt in Tae Kwon Do.
3 There is a clock <u>on the kitchen wall</u>.
4 <u>At the end of my road,</u> there is a playground.
5 I was eating my dinner <u>in the kitchen</u>.

Page 37

Activity 1

> There are lots of opportunities to add adverbials and fronted adverbials! How many did you find?

For example:

… We are planning some exciting improvements <u>for our school</u>.
<u>In the next few weeks,</u> lockers will be fitted <u>in classrooms</u> …
… <u>Over the summer holidays,</u> we are going to redecorate …
… <u>Next year,</u> we will be building a new music and drama studio <u>behind the main school building</u>.
… Finally, we will <u>soon</u> be providing every classroom …

Activity 2

Use this checklist to mark your answer.
My letter …

☐ … uses Standard English
☐ … politely explains the improvements

☐ … includes a greeting and a signoff
☐ … correctly uses at least three fronted adverbials.

Page 39

Activity 1

1 A mighty wind howled and towering waves crashed over the tiny ship. ✔
3 The ancient timbers of the ship creaked and groaned. ✔
5 Tall, ragged cliffs loomed in the distance. ✔

There are three expanded noun phrases in the first sentence!

Activity 2

1 <u>Before the test,</u> Naz felt very nervous.
2 <u>After the test,</u> Naz felt much better.
3 <u>On his farm,</u> the farmer kept a thousand sheep.
4 <u>In his barn,</u> the farmer kept his chickens.
5 <u>On the sailor's shoulder,</u> sat a monkey.

All fronted adverbials are separated by a comma, so make sure you remembered to underline them all.

Page 40

Activity 1

For example:

1 Raz put on <u>his shiny new trainers</u> and headed for the front door.
2 <u>A fierce, fire-breathing dragon with enormous wings</u> flew overhead.
3 Rapunzel let down <u>her long, flowing hair</u>.
4 Scuttling towards me, was <u>a large brown rat with a very long tail</u>.

You could have used adjectives and/or phrases beginning with prepositions to expand the noun phrases.

Activity 2

1 <u>In the morning,</u> we set off on a long cycle ride through the countryside.
2 <u>By the edge of a lake,</u> we sat down for a picnic.
3 <u>At a crossroads,</u> we took a wrong turn.
4 <u>After an hour,</u> we realised we had no idea where we were.
5 <u>Eventually,</u> we found our way home.

These fronted adverbials add information about when and where the events took place.

Page 41

Activity 1

For example:
The <u>Old Brass</u> Lamp
… I have found <u>amazing</u> treasures!"
… the car boot sale <u>at the local football club</u>.
I was trying to watch television <u>in the living room</u>.
… dumped a <u>huge carboard</u> box full of <u>old</u> rubbish <u>right in front of the TV</u>.
… spreading them out <u>on the carpet</u>. There were <u>broken plastic</u> dolls, <u>ancient</u> toys, <u>mouldy, dusty</u> books <u>with torn covers</u> and a <u>dented old brass</u> lamp.
… I could hear Mum groaning <u>loudly</u> …
… <u>A minute or two later</u>, I found myself picking up the <u>old brass</u> lamp. It had some <u>strange and mysterious</u> markings on it …

Activity 2

Use this checklist to mark your answer.
My story …

☐ … explains what happens next

☐ … correctly uses at least three expanded noun phrases

☐ … captures the reader's imagination

☐ … correctly uses at least three adverbials.

Well done if you found some opportunities to add description and detail with noun phrases and adverbials!

        Pinpoint English Grammar and Punctuation Year 4/P5

Page 43

Activity 1

1 A bee flaps its wings about two hundred times every second. ✔
2 This makes a buzzing sound as it flies. ✔
3 Bees fly from flower to flower, collecting the nectar which they will make into honey. ✔

> These three sentences are about bees. The other sentence is about wasps, which is a different topic.

Activity 2

1 "What are you doing for sports day?" asked Max. ☑ "The egg and spoon race," said Alice. ☐ "I'm a champion egg and spoon racer," she added. ☐ "The others won't stand a chance!"

2 Venus is the nearest planet to ours. ☐ It is about the same size as Earth but the temperature on Venus is hot enough to melt lead! ☑ Mars is smaller than Earth. ☐ Some scientists believe there may be some forms of life on this small, red planet. ☐

3 Ellie and I are going to visit Auntie Jan and Uncle Steve next week. ☐ We're really looking forward to seeing them and all the dogs and cats! ☑ Ellie will be starting her new school in September. ☐ I think she is quite excited about it.

Page 44

Activity 1

1 paragraph 1
2 paragraph 2
3 paragraph 1
4 paragraph 1
5 paragraph 2

> Sentences 1, 3 and 4 give a positive view of homework. Sentences 2 and 5 give a negative view of homework.

Activity 2

For example:
1 My favourite book is *Charlie and the Chocolate Factory*. I love it because it is funny and exciting. My favourite character is Willy Wonka.
2 My favourite film is *Frozen*. I love all the different characters because some are funny, some are clever, some are heroes and some are villains. I also love the songs, of course!

Page 45

Activity 1

… It took a quarter of a million different drawings to make the very first full length animation film. *//* … … animators still have to tell them what to do! *//* …

> Each paragraph is about a different type of animation.

Activity 2

Use this checklist to mark your answer.
My report …

☐ … uses formal language

☐ … explains information clearly

☐ … includes facts

☐ … correctly uses at least three paragraphs.

Answers

Page 47

Activity 1

2 Sam asked, "Who's there?" ✔
5 "Don't cry! It's only a joke," said Naveed. ✔

Activity 2

1 "My shoes need to be cleaned," said Griselda.
2 Cindy replied, "But I haven't finished washing your socks yet."
3 "Then you must wash them more quickly," shrieked Griselda.
4 Cindy muttered, "All these stinky socks will take hours to wash."
5 "And your shoes smell even worse than your socks," she added.

> You could also use exclamation marks instead of commas or full stops in some of these sentences. Read your answer carefully and check it makes good sense.

Page 48

Activity 1

For example:

1 "I have created an amazing new invention," said the Professor.
2 "What is it?" asked Tom.
3 "It's a flying robot," said the Professor.
4 "That's amazing! How does it fly?" asked Tom.
5 "I'm not sure yet," said the Professor.

> Did you spot the places where you needed to use a question mark?

Activity 2

1 "Someone has been eating my porridge," said Baby Bear.
2 Priti asked Alfie, "Can I borrow your colouring pencils?"
3 "It's a secret," whispered Jacob.
4 "I'm going to make a cake," said Joe.
5 Katie yelled, "Oh no, I dropped the eggs!"

Page 49

Activity 1

… "Hello, Granny," said Cara.
"Hello, my dear," said Granny.
"I've been looking forward to staying with you for ages," said Cara …
… Granny smiled and said, "Me too. I've got a surprise for you. Come with me."
… "What is it, Granny?" she asked.

> Check you have put each piece of speech in inverted commas.

Activity 2

Use this checklist to mark your answer.
My story …

☐ … explains what happens next

☐ … captures the reader's imagination

☐ … correctly uses at least three pieces of direct speech.

> Check you have got a punctuation mark before the closing speech marks and at the end of the reporting clause.

      Pinpoint English Grammar and Punctuation Year 4/P5

Page 5I

Activity I

I   During the stone age, most humans lived as hunter-gatherers. ☐ This means they did not grow their own food. ☐ They had to go and hunt for meat and gather wild plants. ☑ Stone age people lived in caves.

> The first three sentences are about what stone age humans ate. The last sentence is about where they lived.

2   The King said to Hercules, "You must beat the Hydra. That is your first task." ☑ "How should I beat it?" asked Hercules, feeling nervous. ☐ He waited for the King to reply. ☐ It felt like a very long time.

3   The school concert was a great success. ☐ It was a complete sellout! ☑ Sports day was another highlight of the year. ☐ Every student took part and we all enjoyed the excellent weather.

Activity 2

I   Dee said, "You're late."
2   "I'm starving!" said Bea.
3   "Who's there?" yelled Mani.
4   Ivy said, "Thanks!"

Page 52

Activity I

… without leaving our homes. _//_ …
… an online shop, an online encyclopaedia, or an online game! _//_ …

Activity 2

For example:
I   Amber asked, "Could I have another sandwich?"
2   Chloe's dad asked, "What would you like for dinner?"
3   "Sorry, Mrs Bromley," said Zack.
4   "I will invade England," said Julius Caesar.

> You need to change the pronouns when you turn reported speech into direct speech.

Page 53

Activity I

… even ride on a tractor! _//_
… clambering over each other and bleating. _//_
… Mum asked, "Do you want to be a sheep farmer when you're older?" _//_
"Maybe," I said. _//_

> There should be five paragraphs altogether. How many did you find?

Activity 2

Use this checklist to mark your answer.
My diary entry …

☐   … is in the first person
☐   … correctly uses at least three paragraphs

☐   … uses informal language
☐   … correctly uses at least three pieces of direct speech.

Published by Pearson Education Limited, 80 Strand, London, WC2R 0RL.

www.pearsonschools.co.uk

Text © Pearson Education Limited 2018
Written by David Grant
Edited, typeset and produced by Elektra Media Ltd
Original illustrations © Pearson Education Limited 2018
Illustrated by The Boy Fitz Hammond and Elektra Media Ltd
Cover design and illustration by Eva Caldas

First published 2018

21 20 19 18
10 9 8 7 6 5 4 3 2 1

British Library Cataloguing in Publication Data
A catalogue record for this book is available from the British Library

ISBN 978 1 292 26654 1

Printed in the United Kingdom by Ashford Colour Press Ltd.

Note from the publisher
Pearson has robust editorial processes, including answer and fact checks, to ensure the accuracy of the content in this publication, and every effort is made to ensure this publication is free of errors. We are, however, only human, and occasionally errors do occur. Pearson is not liable for any misunderstandings that arise as a result of errors in this publication, but it is our priority to ensure that the content is accurate. If you spot an error, please do contact us at resourcescorrections@pearson.com so we can make sure it is corrected.